# Bygone
# SEAFORD

## John Odam

ISBN: 978-1-902170-18-3
Originally published in 1990 (ISBN: 0-85033-7356)
Re-published in its original form by Seaford Museum and Heritage Society, 2009.
Printed by Tansleys Printers,
Broad Street, Seaford

Church Street.

*To the delightful Seaford Museum of Local History
(and its totally voluntary committee and members)
without which I would have had neither the inspiration
nor much of the material to make this book possible.*

*This book is written in the hope
that it may stimulate a greater interest in the museum
and a more widespread desire to preserve
Seaford's few remaining buildings of historic or architectural interest.*

# List of Illustrations

## Acknowledgements

Most of the written material for this book is the result of my research into Seaford's history for a long series of articles published in the *Seaford Gazette*. It is difficult in retrospect to be precise as to detailed sources but the main credit must be to our Seaford Museum for many of the facts and most of the old photographs included.

I am grateful to Ordnance Survey and the Public Record Office for permission to include the maps and to the County Record Office at Lewes for the Window Tax record and many facts gleaned from perusal of the minutes of the 17th- and 18th-century meetings of the old Seaford Corporation. Also to the Sussex Archaeological Society for details of Poynings Town and Jack Cade's rebellion and illustration No.59 (S.A.C. vol VII), Ron Steward of Phoenix Corner for numerous postcards and Steyne House Antiques for illustration No.14. I have also had willing help from Seaford Public Library and cheerful expertise from the staff of Island Press.

I would like to thank Roger Hayes for his knowledge and help in compiling the map of 'the era of the private schools' and George Jakens for his enormous enthusiasm which has helped to preserve so much evidence of Seaford's past.

Finally, although some of the pictures in this book are my own or copies of old originals, the credit for many of the final illustrations is due to the patience and skill of Eric Rogers, vice chairman of the Seaford Photographic Society, in producing publishable prints from a wide variety of old photographic negatives.

# Introduction

The history of any place is affected, often dictated, by its geographical location, and there is no better example of this than the town of Seaford. Had it grown up a few miles further north, it would never have been more than a village and would probably have remained less important than neighbouring Alfriston which is sited next to a once navigable river. But men settled in Seaford because it was on the coast and on a river estuary and it is this which has shaped its history at every period since.

Flint implements have been found in and around the town, indicating Stone Age occupation of the area, and part of a large Iron Age hill fort is still discernible on Seaford Head in spite of considerable cliff erosion. There was a substantial Roman villa at Eastbourne and a Roman burial ground on the present Seaford Head golf course. Roman funerary vessels and Roman coins have been found locally so it would seem that Seaford was inhabited periodically, if not constantly, by Ancient Britons right through to the Romano-British period.

The first written evidence of Seaford comes from the Saxon occupation in the fifth century when *Sefordt* was mentioned in early chronicles inferring a ford near the sea or perhaps a fiord of the sea. An eighth-century transaction mentions a town as being *Super fluvium Saforda* or 'on the river Saforda', presumably the river Ouse which then flowed into the sea at Seaford.

Although the town's earliest history must remain vague, the sea and the river Ouse are very real and we do know how nature used these two geographical features to set Seaford literally on the map. In fact, to understand Seaford's eminence in the Middle Ages and its political significance in the 18th century we simply have to look at the winds and tides in Seaford Bay.

Although Seaford is on the south coast, it actually faces south-west so is at the mercy of the gales coming in directly from the Atlantic. Many centuries ago the tides and prevailing winds gradually built up a great shingle bank right across Seaford Bay from the cliffs at Meeching (Newhaven) to the cliffs at Seaford Head. As this barrier grew, the river Ouse was diverted eastwards until it drove its way out into the sea at Splash Point under Seaford Head and the very low-lying area behind the bank was flooded and formed a natural harbour.

It is difficult to picture this in the Seaford of today until one remembers that in Saxon times the cliff ends at Meeching and Seaford projected much further out into the sea, so that the shingle barrier was considerably further seaward than the present shoreline. A look at the conjectural map of the bay in that period superimposed over Seaford of the 1980s shows how the old river Ouse flowed inland, rounding the spurs and lapping into the ancient Ice Age valleys of Bishopstone, Hawth and Blatchington. (See illustration No.2)

Certainly this happened long before the Norman Conquest and we know that by the early 13th century Seaford was a Cinque Port and senior limb of the head port of Hastings, the other head ports at that time being Sandwich, Dover, Romney and Hythe. During its most prosperous period the port of Seaford gave employment in fishing, ship building, provisioning of ships and a two-way trade with the continent, importing wines and exporting wool from the large flocks of Downland sheep.

A busy port also needed defence so there was a fort to protect its entrance and presumably some form of local militia to man it. The entire maritime defence of the realm was in the hands of the Cinque Ports whose duty it was to provide a tally of ships and 'marines' proportionate to their respective status. It is known that in 1342 Seaford sent three ships to the French wars and in 1347 its official tally was five ships and 80 marines, so it is not difficult to picture a bustling port and a thriving populous town in the 14th century. In 1298, because it was a Cinque Port, Seaford was granted the right to send two members to parliament. This had a great influence on its political and social history over the next 500 years.

Although Seaford shares with London, Bristol and Liverpool the rare distinction of *not* being mentioned in Domesday Book, we know that in the 12th and early 13th centuries the town was in the lordship of the Earls de Warenne and then passed to Michael Lord

Poynings, but the separate Manor of Chington (now Chyngton, and variously spelt Chingting, Chyngting, Chyntinge etc.) was owned by the de Aquila family. This helps to explain the Seaford coat of arms which shows, *dexter*, the two half lions/half ships from the arms of Hastings; *sinister*, the eagle from the Aquila arms and base, the ship from the arms of the Cinque Ports. The motto, *E Ventis Vires*, 'strength from the winds', has proved very significant in Seaford's chequered history.

As a Cinque Port Seaford was granted a charter by Henry VIII which confirms and embodies all the duties and privileges it enjoyed since its inception as a town, parish and borough. These privileges excused its members from various national duties and allowed the borough to be more or less self-governing locally, with its own corporation. The corporation consisted of freemen, jurats and a bailiff. The bailiff was elected annually on Michaelmas Day by the freemen. The freemen and jurats were nominated and elected by the corporation. The bailiff could only serve for one year at a time so we find the same local families succeeding each other in and out of office in a continuous merry-go-round over the centuries!

The bailiff and jurats administered the law and the old town hall in South Street had its own jail under the court house. Minutes of corporation meetings and fines and punishments awarded were kept from 1562 right up until 1886 and can still be viewed, page by page and year by year, in the County Record Office. These records show sentences ranging from fines and periods in the stocks or pillory, to duckings, whippings, branding and transportation, all administered in the little town, with only more heinous cases being sent to the county assizes.

In spite of its early prosperity, the town was in decline by the second half of the 14th century. By 1380, as a result of the plague and of raids by parties of Frenchmen burning and looting, the people of Seaford were petitioning Richard II for relief from their taxes. By 1400, they could no longer pay the expenses of their two members of parliament and their electoral rights elapsed for 241 years.

During this time the sea had continued to shift the shingle eastward, gradually restricting the mouth of the harbour. Gales were threatening to drive the sea across the shingle bank and flood the town, so in 1421 Robert Lord Poynings and Sir John Pelham were commissioned to investigate repairs to the whole bank across Seaford Bay. Their efforts must have been in vain for by 1439 the town was unable to pay its usual church tithes because of floods, inundations and conflagrations. About this time, in a remarkable example of early town planning, Lord Poynings attempted to replace the ravaged old town on Seaford Bay by a new settlement on the eastern slopes of Seaford Head overlooking the more tranquil Cuckmere estuary. This was shown near Chyngton Farm on the old Ordnance Survey maps of 1873 as 'Poynings Town' and 'Walls Brow'. (See illustration No.4) Traces of foundations and walls were still visible in the mid-19th century to the Victorian historian Mark Anthony Lower who observed consistent traces of burning, suggesting that the embryo township was probably destroyed by fire. Aerial photographs taken in 1967 over Poynings Town and Walls Brow show clear signs of the presence of earlier buildings, now mostly invisible at ground level, and would seem to substantiate what for about four centuries was little more than a legend. (See illustration No.6)

Perhaps because of the sorry state of the old town of Seaford, in 1450 Richard Carpenter, then bailiff, and seven yeomen, one butcher and one barber of the town, together with Robert Poynings of Sutton, all took an active part in Jack Cade's rebellion. This was an uprising of the yeoman class against the taxes of the Lancastrian King Henry VI and in support of the exiled Duke of York, a foretaste of the Wars of the Roses a few years later. All the Seaford men are individually named in the pardons later granted on condition that they returned peaceably to their homes.

The relentless pressures of the sea continued to shift the shingle bank until in the mid-16th century the harbour mouth was almost unnavigable and the whole of the wide Ouse valley up towards Lewes was so wet or flooded as to be almost worthless. Although it was said that a great storm caused a dramatic change, it is more logical to accept that the people (possibly assisted by nature) cut a new outlet for the river at the village of Meeching, thus forming the New Haven. This gradually ruined Seaford as a harbour although fishing rights were still being granted for the land-locked 'old haven' as late as 1728 and a map of c.1736 clearly shows large areas of waterways inside the shingle bank. (See illustration No.3)

In 1545 a small French fleet attempting to land in Seaford Bay was repulsed by the men of the town and local landowners under the leadership of Sir Nicholas Pelham whose family has had an influence over much of Seaford's history and whose coat of arms, a 'buckle', gives its name to the area where this 16th-century action took place.

With the harbour and its consequent trade gone, the fortunes of the town declined even further and in 1596 there were said to be only 38 householders, including seven fishermen with only one boat. In 1592 the harbour was so decayed that Queen Elizabeth I made a gift of the low-lying land around the old haven, now known as the Beame Lands, to the people of Seaford in perpetuity.

As Newhaven developed as a harbour and small ships could navigate to and trade in Lewes, the harbour mouth was progressively extended with protective moles built out into the sea but this so upset the tidal forces that the constant drift of shingle was disturbed. The great barrier which had formed Seaford harbour and later silted up its exit now began to be scoured away and left the town at even greater risk of flooding from high tides and storms.

Although remaining nominally a Cinque Port and retaining its corporation, there was little employment and no incentive towards growth of population until in 1641, just before the Civil War, Seaford surprisingly regained its right to send two members to parliament. It is probable that the town was known to be parliamentarian at that time and that its votes would be an asset. Certainly its two members were 'secluded' from parliament at the restoration of the monarchy. However, once its franchise was re-established new jobs appeared in Seaford in the form of service on the lands and in the houses of the wealthy landowners who found 'jobs for the boys' in return for votes. As a coastal town, most of the jobs or 'places' (other than domestic posts) were related to customs and excise, some involving actual work but some just sinecures requiring little or no duties beyond voting as required at elections.

In most country districts politics were controlled by the local landed gentry. Although Seaford, Blatchington and Sutton had families which might have formed a squirearchy, they were totally overshadowed in the 18th century by the powerful Pelham family which had vast estates in various counties including property at Laughton, a few miles north of Seaford. As Seaford was one of what came to be known as the 'rotten boroughs', where a handful of electors voted for two members of parliament, it was a tempting political prize and the Pelhams kept Bishopstone Place as a base from which to direct and control the voters of Seaford, using the local gentry and placemen (sinecure holders) as their agents.

We have an interesting insight into property in Seaford from the window tax record of 1713/14 – one of only two known records of this old tax in the whole of Sussex. Before the days of income tax this was a simple toll levied on each house according to its number of windows. Capt. Harison, John Goldham and Robert Palmer, all bailiffs at various times, each had over 20 windows; 11 houses had between 10 and 20 windows, 17 houses had between six and ten windows; and humble cottages of less than six windows were untaxed, so apart from a very small upper crust, the people of the town in 1714 were moderate in their means and modest in their aspirations. (See illustration No.7)

In 1712 Thomas Pelham-Holles succeeded his father as 2nd Baron Pelham and later became Duke of Newcastle with numerous other titles and distinctions. He came of age in 1714 and, after an enormous banquet in celebration, he took his seat in the House of Lords to influence and later dominate the nation's politics almost to his death in 1768. It is hardly surprising that he used his 'pocket borough' of Seaford to good advantage.

The duke had a major-domo at Bishopstone Place – Thomas Swaine, whose family ran the *Old Tree Inn* at Seaford (an excellent sounding-board for local gossip). His private secretary was Thomas Hurdis D.D., nominally vicar of Seaford for 35 years, whose son was for some time curate in charge of the parish. With his other 'placemen' it is not difficult to see how the duke kept a very firm grip on the political pulse of the town.

In those days there was no secret ballot and on election day, having been liberally wined and dined (if minor gentry), or given plenty of ale and a good tip, the voters had to assemble in the old town hall and stand up under the stern eye of the duke and voice their vote. They naturally put their vote where their jobs and their financial interests lay, thus ensuring continued employment around Seaford for years to come!

As a result of this system the duke's younger brother, Henry Pelham, was elected together with other useful friends and members of the family until in 1750 George II said of the duke, his brother Henry, then Prime Minister, and the Lord Chancellor (originally elected for Seaford): 'They are the only Ministers, the others are for show'. William Pitt and George Canning also became Prime Ministers after representing Seaford in parliament.

Occasionally there were contesting candidates, including the Gage family of Firle, which led to rival feasting and suitable inducements on the eve of elections and then to petitions to parliament and debates in the House of Commons on the conduct of elections in Seaford, but the Pelham faction invariably won.

The debate always turned on precisely which of the town's inhabitants were entitled to vote. This depended on who paid 'Scot and Lot', or the forerunner of local rates. In the 18th century there was a noticeable tendency in Seaford to apply to be rated just before a general election with its potential handouts, and then a rush to be de-rated when the spoils were won and elections over for a few years!

The matter of voting entitlement also sparked off occasional trouble in the election of the bailiff. Two cases were taken to the high court in 1763 and 1764 involving the elections of Robert Stone and Thomas Washer, when the populace claimed that they had not been properly represented. In 1775 in an attempt to displace the bailiff, Lancelot Harison, the court house was invaded, a shoemaker took away the town chest with its records and there was almost a reading of the Riot Act before order was restored. In 1789 there was another riot at the town hall inspired by T. H. B. Oldfield, a political reformer, no doubt with an eye to the main chance.

Politics were not the only reason for conflict locally and some of the people of Seaford gained the sobriquet of 'Shags' or 'Cormorants', not only for their propensity for smuggling and looting of the many ships wrecked in or near the bay, but also for the more dastardly crime of using lights to entice ships onto the foreshore or cliffs and then to help themselves to any cargo they could salvage.

Wrecks from natural causes were common enough in the days of sail and the early days of steam. No sailor likes to be too close to a lee shore and coming up channel with southerly gales or easterly headwinds made the rounding of Beachy Head most hazardous. So it was not uncommon to find great numbers of ships anchored in the comparative safety of Seaford Bay, sometimes for days, awaiting more favourable conditions. This bay was not always a safe haven – in 1809 an 18-gun naval sloop, along with the six merchant ships it was escorting, stood into the bay at night thinking they had already rounded Beachy Head and all seven ships foundered on the shore.

Although 18th-century Seaford was closely bound up with politics and its financial advantages, the main occupation outside the town was still agricultural. The river Ouse no longer flowed through Seaford, but in 1761 the Duke of Newcastle enabled the building of corn grinding mills on a still tidal creek of the old river on the coast opposite Bishopstone. These tide mills were driven by water wheels powered by the tide rising into a mill pond and again by the ebb tide flowing out from the pond. They gave considerable employment and an almost autonomous village was built on the site to house the workers. Later there were windmills at Blatchington and Sutton but the tide mills survived until steam power made this little local industry redundant.

During the Napoleonic Wars Seaford Bay was potentially an excellent landing place for a French invasion and again it had to be defended. There was a small battery at Splash Point and another to the west of the town. As bailiff in 1794 Thomas Harben, who in 1783 had transported the original 'Corsica Hall' by barge from Wellingham to Seaford, raised a local volunteer defence force. In the same year a tented camp of the Wiltshire Militia at Seaford was almost completely blown away one night in a sudden rain storm and barracks were built at Blatchington, where later there was a mutiny caused by wretched conditions and worse food.

Martello Tower No.74, the last of a chain of similar forts stretching round the coast from the Thames estuary, was completed in 1808, but with Nelson's victory at Trafalgar in 1805 the serious risk of invasion was removed and Seaford's defences were never put to the test.

After the death of the Duke of Newcastle in 1768 local politics were sometimes contentious but the large-scale distribution of sinecures ceased. Later, as a result of the 1832 Reform Bill, Seaford finally lost its franchise and so became of little value to political landowners and the town again faced the prospect of decline for want of employment.

In 1799, on the eve of the 19th century, a sad indication of the state of the little town is found in the records with a note that 'the Jury found a True Bill of Nuisance against the Hog Pounds in the West Lanes, the dung heaps between the Post Office and the Ship Inn and also from the Dark Lane to the piece of land called the Crouch'. In 1814 the town had 153 houses occupied by 181 families consisting of 464 males and 537 females. Two houses were being built and, surprisingly, seven houses were uninhabited!

Along the coast the little town of Brighthelmstone had blossomed due to the interest of the future George IV, into the beginnings of the fashionable seaside resort of Brighton. Could Seaford exploit its seaboard to bring prosperity in a similar way?

Unfortunately the sea which had created the town was still its frequent enemy and in 1824 a great storm broke through the shingle bank between Splash Point and the Martello Tower, and also near the western battery. This not only flooded the lower part of the town but washed inland along the old valleys almost to Blatchington pond and carried a barge right up past Bishopstone church almost to the next hamlet of Norton, temporarily reproducing the waterways shown in illustration No.2.

In 1835 Lord Palmerston was petitioned for a new harbour to be made in Seaford Bay at government expense but the estimated costs proved prohibitive. In 1850, in an attempt to prevent further erosion of the protective shingle bank, sappers were employed to mine into the chalk cliffs of Seaford Head and explode 11 tons of gunpowder. This dislodged 380,000 tons of chalk onto the foreshore intended as a barrier to restrain the tidal drift. Unfortunately, although great crowds flocked to watch this exciting spectacle – including Charles Dickens – the great expectations were mocked by the sea which washed away the chalk almost more quickly than the shingle.

In spite of this, in 1857 Dr. Tyler-Smith (who later became bailiff) set up The Seaford Improvement Committee. From small beginnings this inspired the concept of a seaside resort, encouraged the extension of the railway which came to Seaford in 1864, and built up Pelham Road with its rather dour urban Victorian terraces in a still largely rural 18th-century and earlier township.

A proper sea wall was started in 1865 but it was destroyed in another disastrous storm in 1875 when the town was again badly flooded, though the railway embankment this time prevented the floods making inroads as far as they had in 1824. In 1880 a petition signed by 44 inhabitants was given to William Webb Turner, bailiff, calling for measures to render the town presentable and attractive to visitors.

In 1885 the last bailiff of Seaford was elected and the ancient corporation, which had existed for 600 years and whose detailed records are extant for its last 300 years, sadly and abruptly came to an end to be replaced by a Local Board and then in 1894 by the totally unromantic Seaford Urban District Council.

Various companies were set up to try to develop the town as a resort. A better, but far from impregnable, sea wall was built, the elevated roadways from the Steyne to the sea front were constructed, and the promenade and the first terraced houses were built facing the sea including in 1891 the *Esplanade Hotel*, the flagship of the enterprise. In 1905 Edward VII honoured Seaford by staying in the *Esplanade Hotel*. The town was aiming to imitate Brighton, but the entrepreneurial Seaford Bay Estate Company had overlooked the rigours of Seaford's winter gales and their few seaside homes and lodgings were never to prove commercially viable.

The Company's proposed developments were very grandiose and the whole area from Splash Point to the present end of Dane Road was planned on the lines of Brighton with 12 parallel roads of terraced houses running back in serried rows from the Esplanade to College Road and Steine Road (*sic*) only relieved by a miniature 'Royal Crescent' on the centre line of the Martello Tower. Behind this, Cricket Field was to be flanked on the north and east by 22 seaside bungalows (of three storeys!), nine of which were actually built before the company went bankrupt and any further permanent development subsided under the threat and eventual demands of the Great War. (See illustration No.8)

In an Edwardian guide to the town the *Esplanade Hotel* is extolled as being a very handsome and ornate building with over 50 rooms, and 'furnished in *recherché* style'. There were also the less prestigious *Bay Hotel* in Pelham Road and the *New Inn*, which became the *Wellington Hotel*, and several other lesser hotels and boarding houses. There were bathing machines 'of the most improved style', boats for hire, and yacht trips in the bay. Later the old Martello Tower offered 'teas and refreshments' and roller skating round its dry moat, so the town did a reasonable trade in the summer season. The grand development, however, was dead. There was not the demand for yet another resort in the 20 miles of coast between Brighton and Eastbourne, and Seaford, having lost its Duke of Newcastle, was in no position to vie with 'Prinny' or the Duke of Devonshire – the patrons of its more prosperous neighbours.

The *Esplanade Hotel* survived for about 80 years and the rumbustious old town took on a more genteel aspect, but it somehow became more withdrawn. The sea front remained half developed and half derelict and, without the right atmosphere, the entrepreneurial spirit also died.

Although Seaford never really developed as a holiday town its sea air was respected and its restorative powers were exploited in the building, between 1870 and 1901, of several convalescent homes ranging in size from Talland House, on a domestic scale, in High Street to the Seaside Convalescent Home which resembled a typical Victorian Hospital.

During the Great War two vast camps, the North Camp around the present North Way, and South Camp between the present Chyngton Road and Sutton Avenue, housed hundreds of troops and a number who survived the war returned to marry and live in Seaford. The old tide mills site was a seaplane base in the First World War and was used for close quarter battle training in the Second World War when the whole of the sea front was a restricted area in anticipation of another invasion.

West House, one of the earliest Seaford houses still standing, had been a school when Mr. Bull its proprietor had to move to Broad Street after the floods of 1875. This school for young gentlemen was an early forerunner of things to come for, although the town never became a real resort, the healthy air which had encouraged the convalescent homes also inspired 'the era of the private boarding schools'.

In the 20th century, starting in 1903 with Newlands (1905 in its present site), one after another private school bought land around the old town until by the Second World War there were over 20 schools with their requisite playing fields almost dominating the environs of the town. (See illustration No.10)

During the inter-war years and for some time after, these schools were quite a powerful influence on the town because their supplies, maintenance and transport created need for jobs in times of slump and unemployment when Seaford had no other 'industry'. Because of their importance and benefaction to the town, the schools were represented on the Urban District Council, and because they shaped the religious outlook of their charges they also combined to supplement the stipend of the Seaford vicars. Quite apart from these benefits, the schools' playing fields guaranteed breathing spaces of open land within a slowly developing town.

These boarding schools had comparatively small numbers of pupils and parents from a very wide catchment area whose journeys to visit their offspring ended at the coast. When motoring replaced the earlier train journeys, the very poor main roads to Seaford and heavy weekend traffic became a discouragement. As school running costs escalated so did the need to increase the fees. An alternative was to increase numbers of pupils, but this meant buying more land when the costs were rising and risking large capital outlay on a shrinking and politically unsettled market. So, one after another, all but a few of the schools closed, to be snapped up by developers who saturated those green and pleasant lands often with more houses than the number of pupils they replaced.

This brief account of Seaford's interesting history began with the influence of the winds and the sea upon the town's fortunes; from a Cinque Port to a Rotten Borough, to a would-be resort and a healthy place for convalescents and school children. Before the need for conservation was realised most of the historic town's more ancient buildings were pulled down to make way for uninspiring modern shops and houses.

Paradoxically, the cause of the transformation of this once proud borough into an insignificant sprawl was again the sea air. It was this which prompted the development of the many warden-assisted homes and hundreds of retirement houses and bungalows which now totally swamp the old town. Some of the older buildings which have survived have now been 'listed' and it is hoped will be preserved, but photographs of many of these are included in this book as a reminder of their importance to the town as a symbol of continuity.

# Maps & Documents

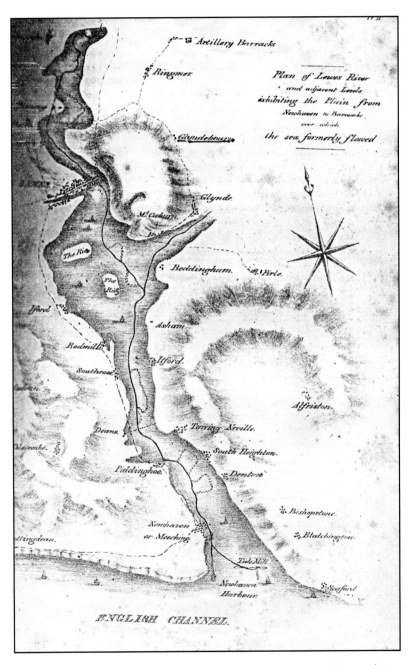

Plan of Lewes River
and adjacent Levels
exhibiting the Plain from
Newhaven to Barcombe
over which
the sea formerly flowed

1.   The river Ouse, from the Rev. Horsfield's *History and Antiquities of Lewes and its vicinities* (1824). This indicates the wide delta of the river before the shingle barrier narrowed its egress at Seaford and formed the inland harbour.

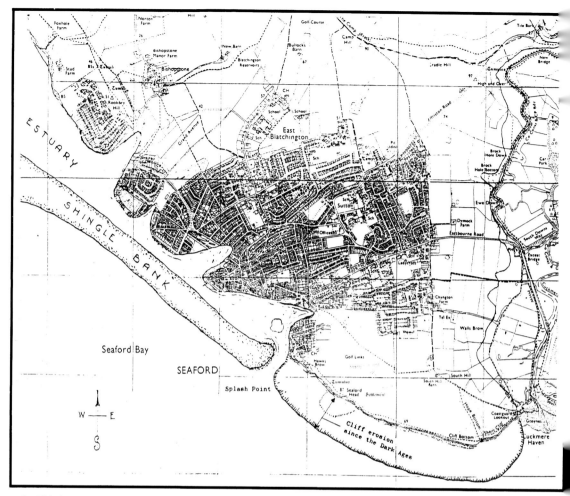

2. This is a conjectural map (drawn by the author) of Seaford Bay showing the great shingle bank of the Dark Ages superimposed upon Seaford of the 1980s. It shows how the old Cinque Port was created and why the sea again flooded into the Ice Age valleys of Bishopstone, Hawth and Blatchington in the great storms of later centuries.

3. Seaford, c.1736 (Public Record Office MR/915/5). Detail from a map of Sussex from Rye to Chichester, copied by F. Gould from an original by an unknown cartographer. Although the town plan is very recognisable and waterways of the 'old haven' are shown, the cartographer has sadly mistaken the angle of the coast in relation to the old town (see Map 4).

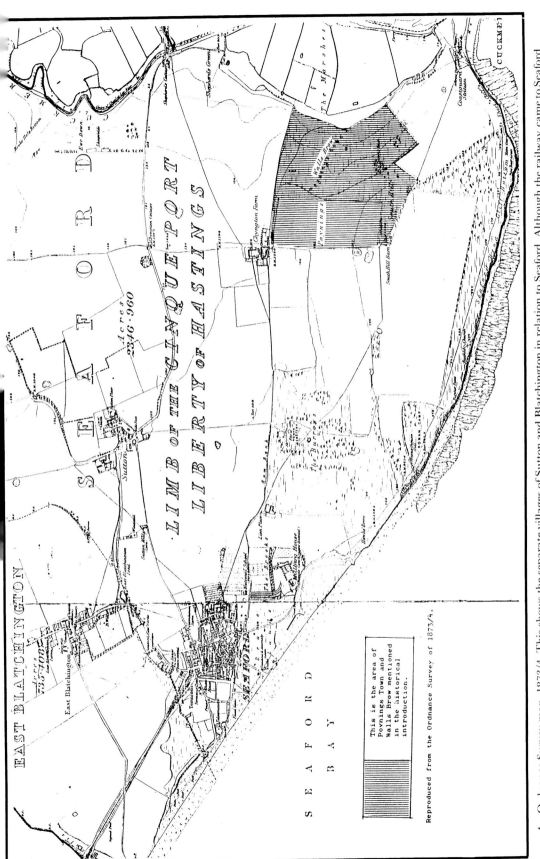

4. Ordnance Survey map, 1873/4. This shows the separate villages of Sutton and Blatchington in relation to Seaford. Although the railway came to Seaford in 1864 there is still very little development beyond the medieval town and the plan of 1736. Note 'Poynings Town', also shown in No.6.

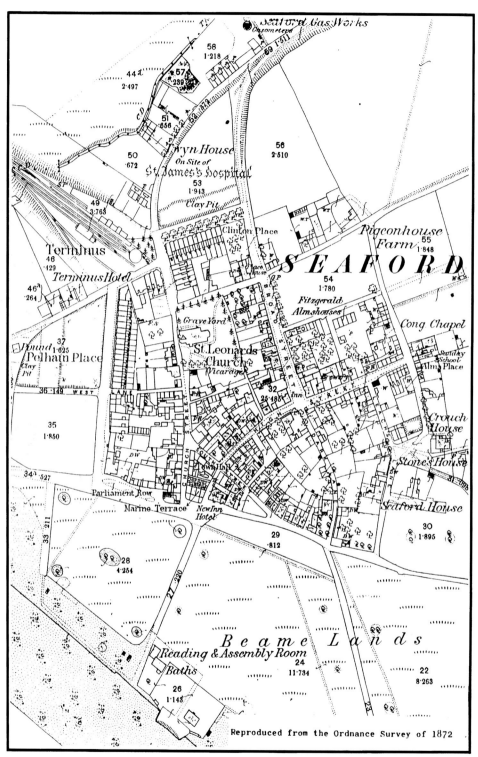

5. Seaford town centre from the 1872 O.S. map. This shows individual buildings and helps to identify many of the later illustrations.

6. Aerial photograph, 1967. The centre of this picture shows the area of Poynings Town and Walls Brow as outlined in Map 4. Chyngton Farm and the modern concrete road are on the left of the site. Distinct traces of field paths and old building foundations seem to confirm that Lord Poynings did at least start a new settlement here in the 15th century.

Suffex Seafoard Window Tax Commencing att Lady Day
1713 to Lady Day 1714 both Old and New Duty &c

| | Windo only | Old Duty | Newdaty |
| --- | --- | --- | --- |
| Capt. Jnº Harrison | 30 | 10 | 20 |
| Jnº Godham Esqr | 26 | 10 10 | |
| Robt Palmer | 26 | 10 10 | |
| Thos Wood | 18 | 6 | |
| James Chambers | 19 | 6 | |
| Stephen Pellington | 18 | 6 | |
| Edwd Flecker | 18 | 6 | |
| Thos Boole | 11 | 6 | |
| Edwd Pellington or Henry Beane | 15 | 6 | |
| Witt Swaine | 16 | 6 | |
| Charles Wood | 11 | 6 | |
| Jnº Tiltman | 6 | 2 | |
| Thos Skinner | 18 | 6 | |
| Jnº Pilbeane | 9 | 2 | |
| Wid: Tufton | 9 | 0 | |
| Jnº Hughs | 7 | 2 | |
| Jnº Austin | 7 | 2 | |
| Will: Tiltman | 16 | 6 | |
| Jnº Holkham | 16 | 6 | |
| Thos Symons | 7 | 2 | |
| Will: Heasell | 8 | 2 | |
| Jnº Brazier | 9 | 2 | |
| Jnº Wood | 8 | 2 | |
| Will: Hubberd | 8 | 2 | |
| Richd Dunton | 9 | 2 | |
| Jnº Dunstone sen | 9 | 2 | |
| James Wood or Thos Washer | 8 | 2 | |
| Thos Tiltman | 8 | 2 | |
| Jnº Jolline | 7 | 2 | |
| Thos Mockurtt and James Wood | 8 | 2 | |
| Richd Ellis | 6 | 2 | |
| Thos Washer per next Rate | | | |

2. 6. 10. 10. 10

16:12:3. 2:1

Examined R. Scrivener surveyor both 8:14

Old Duty 6:14
New Duty 2:00
8:14

Thos Symons } assessors
Richd Dunton }

Wee Nominate

Jnº Holkham } Collectrs
Richd: Ellis }

Allowed by us

Signed and Seald the 23d day of March 1713

John Godham Robt Palmer
James Chambers

7. Seaford window tax, 1713/14. This is one of only two known records of this old tax in the whole of Sussex. Note the mistake made for the Widow Tufton who lived at the Old House in High Street and whose husband had died while bailiff of Seaford in 1712. The top three names appear regularly as bailiffs; several of the others were freemen of the town and corporation.

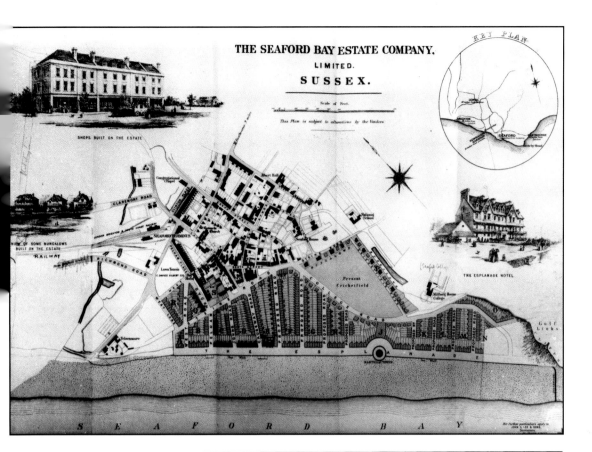

8. Seaford Bay Estate Company Limited. In this grandiose scheme for development the shops on the west of Pelham Road failed and the pier never materialised. Only a few of the houses on the Esplanade and nine of the 'bungalows' round Cricket Field were ever built. The *Esplanade Hotel* was really the only lasting monument to this would-be entrepreneurial exercise.

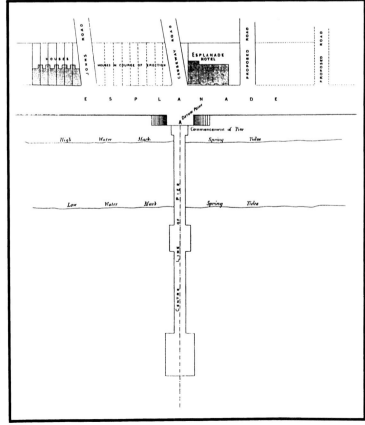

9. Seaford's proposed pier. This drawing was made for the parliamentary sessions of 1893/4. The pier was never built but, as it would have been as wide and as long as Broad Street with two areas twice as wide, would it have influenced Seaford towards a rowdy Brighton or a demure Eastbourne?

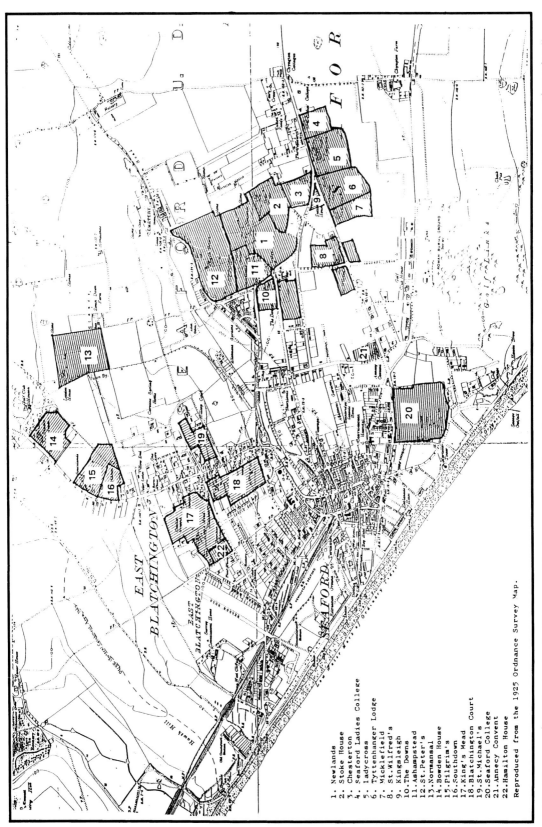

1. Newlands
2. Stoke House
3. Chesterton
4. Seaford Ladies College
5. Ladycross
6. Tyttenhanger Lodge
7. Micklefield
8. St.Wilfred's
9. Kingsleigh
10. The Downs
11. Ashampstead
12. St.Peter's
13. Normansal
14. Bowden House
15. Pilgrim's
16. Southdown
17. King's Mead
18. Blatchington Court
19. St.Michael's
20. Seaford College
21. Annecy Convent
22. Hamilton House

Reproduced from the 1925 Ordnance Survey Map.

10. The era of the private schools. This map of the inter-war years shows the many private schools and how they jointly occupied a total of 'greenland' equal to the whole of the 'developed' area of Seaford at that time.

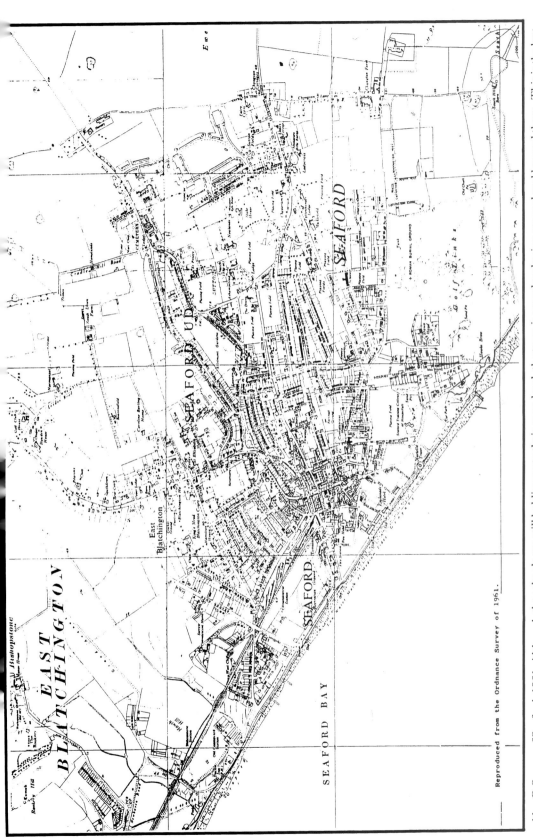

11. O.S. map of Seaford, 1961. Although the schools are still holding onto their open land, the town is now developing around and beyond them. This is the last published Ordnance Survey map before housing development exploded to engulf the outer reaches of the town and infill most of the precious breathing spaces within.

Reproduced from the Ordnance Survey map of 1961.

# The Sea Shore

12. Blowing out the cliffs, 1850. Crowds are watching from the safety of Newhaven as gunpowder mined into Seaford Head cliffs was exploded to cause huge falls of chalk onto the foreshore to contain the eastward shift of the shingle bank. Charles Dickens wrote an article about this which he called 'Powder and Chalk'.

13. After the explosion people crowded over the thousands of tons of chalk blown out of the cliffs. Sadly the chalk was too powdery and was all washed away by the waves and tides within a few months.

14. Seaford in 1785, viewed from the shingle bank, from a painting by S. H. Grimm. Waters of the old harbour still remain in front of West House and Parliament Row. On the horizon, to the left of St Leonard's church, can be seen the spire of St Peter's and the windmill at Blatchington.

15. An engraving of Seaford from the sea. In the foreground is Telsemaure. In the centre is Pelham Road with West House, the *Bay Hotel* and early terraced houses, but the Bay Estate Company had not yet built along the sea front. This view is more or less contemporary with No.16.

*Seaford looking East.*

16. From Splash Point looking west, *c.*1865. In the foreground is the Martello Tower, then, very foreshortened by the camera lens, are the gun battery and quarters, then Telsemaure (built in 1860 by the Crook family) and then the coastguard buildings with the beach sweeping round to Newhaven.

17. The sea front looking west, *c.*1875. This view shows Millberg House (Corsica Hall), the Assembly Rooms (1770) and the Martello Tower. With no sea wall, the shingle bank was very vulnerable to breaching by the sea as in the floods of 1824 and 1875.

18. Baths and Assembly Rooms. Viewed from the landward side, these look much larger than in Plate 17 where they are lost in the vast expanse of shingle.

19. The site of the old haven. This picture, taken around the turn of the century, shows the low-lying land between the Martello and Millberg House. Without the Victorian causeways up from the old town it is easy to picture this whole area deeper and full of water right through to the Salts and beyond.

20. A sketch of the Martello Tower, showing the footbridge across a small watery ditch, as on Map 4. The tower was to be used in conjunction with other batteries in the bay but its dry moat and drawbridge made it a better bastion against assault.

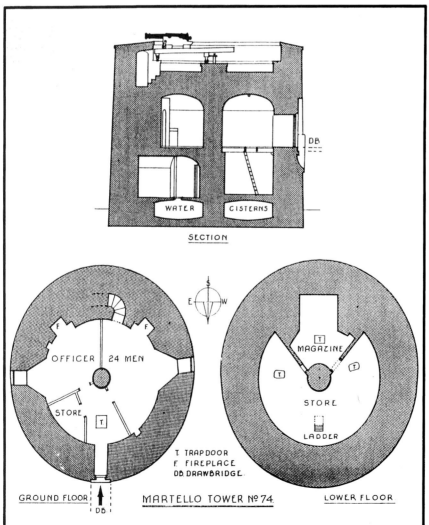

SECTION

DB

WATER    CISTERNS

GROUND FLOOR

F    F
OFFICER | 24 MEN

STORE

T

DB

LOWER FLOOR

MAGAZINE
T
T    T

STORE

LADDER

T. TRAPDOOR
F. FIREPLACE
DB. DRAWBRIDGE

MARTELLO TOWER № 74

E — S — W

21. Plans and section through the Seaford Martello Tower (measured and drawn by the author) as it was constructed in 1806-8 to help repel invasion by the forces of Napoleon. It is now the Seaford Museum of Local History and the drawbridge door and traces of the original windows and fireplaces can be seen.

22. The Buckle Road, looking back towards the old coastguards' quarters (seen distantly in Plate 16). This was the only road out of Seaford to Newhaven and the west until the 1960s! With the sea pounding in, this road was completely impassable.

23. Another view of this only road to the west (except by the long route back via Alfriston and the A27). Note the danger sign – *Ca va sans dire*!

24. Portrait of Sir Nicholas Pelham painted four years after he led the rout of a landing by the French in 1545. The buckle in his coat of arms, dating from the battle of Poitiers, gives its name to an area of Seaford Bay.

25. The *Buckle*, *c*.1913. This card was posted in 1920 but probably printed before 1914. On a calm day like this the sea wall is clearly visible, but it is barely discernible in the next picture.

26.   A picture of the *Buckle* taken in a storm in 1924.

27.   Repairing damage from the 1924 storm. This was exactly 100 years after the great floods of 1824 when a barge was swept from the beach right up Bishopstone valley, past the church and almost to the hamlet of Norton.

28.   The *Esplanade Hotel*, *c*.1892 – the pride of the Seaford Bay Estate Company and just as it was built in 1891 with the diminutive Assembly Rooms dwarfed alongside.

29.   The *Esplanade Hotel*, *c*.1895, looking west and now with posts presumably to protect guests from horse vehicles in front of the hotel or dashing along the promenade.

30.  This early advertisement for 'A modern hotel *replete* with every 19th century convenience' shows some artistic licence in its apparent proximity to Seaford Head and its height in relation to the 200-ft. cliffs!

31.  The hotel after completion. Now the old Assembly Rooms have been replaced by an even larger west wing with three tiers of dormer windows in its steep roof. Carriage traffic is restored with a proper road and pavements.

32. The old town from the Esplanade. In the foreground can be seen one of the derelict causeways and the Methodist church and beyond, from the left, the Steyne from Marine Terrace round to the battlement walls of Saxon Lodge.

33. Looking north across Cricket Field. At the top right is the Seaside Convalescent Hospital and in front are four of the bungalows. One of the nine bungalows built at that time still exists in 1989, on the east corner of Cricket Field and Steyne Road.

34. The Steyne looking east, before the road was made up or the 'bungalows' were built around Cricket Field.

35. The Steyne, c.1900. By this date the road is made up with a pavement and nine of the bungalows have been completed, although the Bay Estate Co. never built any more of the 22 shown on their plan (Plate 8).

36.  The Seaside Convalescent Hospital, established in 1860. This was the first convalescent hospital built in this country to give sea air, rest and a good diet to restore poor patients (after long illnesses in city hospitals) to sufficient strength to return to work.

37.  The Bainbridge convalescent home. This building had been the Swiss Pavilion at the 1900 Paris Exhibition and was bought and erected by the Bainbridge family for poor girls from large towns and was later run by the Y.W.C.A. It can be seen on Map 10 at the east end of Crouch Fields.

38.  Appeal for the convalescent hospital. Three Dukes, three Earls, one Viscount, two Princesses, two Duchesses, one Marchioness, two Countesses, one Viscountess, a Lord, a Lady and the Archbishop of Canterbury were impeccable patrons of this innovative Seaford enterprise.

39. Surrey convalescent home. With similar aims to the Seaside Convalescent Hospital, this was built in 1888 on 10 acres of land about 200 yards north of the railway (see Map 10). It survived until the 1960s but would have been right alongside the new Buckle by-pass.

40.  The *New Inn* before it was renamed the *Wellington Hotel*, with Marine Terrace and the Steyne. The drinking fountain in pink marble and wrought iron commemorates Queen Victoria's Jubilee of 1887.

41.  The *Wellington*, renamed many years after the possibly apochryphal visit of the famous Duke. Note the billiards and smoking rooms and in the background 'Wood's Grocers' at the bottom of High Street.

# MAZAWATTEE
## HIGH-CLASS TEA.

TEA is without doubt the most popular national beverage used by the British public. It engenders feelings of thankfulness and hope, promoting thoughts of peace and good-will towards our fellows.

It therefore behoves us to take every precaution to ensure that we get **Tea that is Tea,** and not an injurious and unpalatable substitute which will produce effects the reverse of those described.

Better by far have **one cup of good Tea** a week than insult our palates and ruin our tempers and digestions by drinking rubbish daily.

To meet this long-felt want **The Mazawattee Ceylon Tea Company** was founded. The Company have nothing whatever to do with **Common Tea,** knowing it to be dear at any price.

The great **secret** of their **success** is that the Public **have** found out that the

## Mazawattee Teas
### Recall the delicious China Teas of
# THIRTY YEARS AGO.

Prices—1/10, 2/-, 2/4, 2/10, and 4/- per lb.

**In One-pound, Half-pound and Quarter-pound Lead Packets, and in Three-pound and Six-pound Tins.**

Sold by leading Grocers throughout the United Kingdom.

**Agent for Seaford:**

## W. B. WOOD, Family Grocer, High Street.

42. A contemporary advertisement for the family grocer. Its bland naivety of style is interesting, as are the details of the price of tea and the lead packets.

43.   A later view of the *Wellington*, after refurbishment. Because the roadway was narrowed by the Methodist church and its railings opposite, the drinking fountain was moved to the Salts where it now languishes, derelict, without its lamp and wrought-iron work.

# The Railway

*The Railway Terminus, Seaford.*

44. Seaford Railway Terminus. The railway reached Seaford in 1864 and this is probably a contemporary engraving. Beyond the essential turntable can be seen the *Terminus Hotel* between the ends of Clinton Place and Pelham Place (see Map 5).

45. The line into Seaford (see Map 4). The station approach was only a short cul-de-sac on the railway embankment for years before this was extended to meet the new Claremont Road. Before the railway embankment was built up the sea could, and sometimes did, sweep across the Salts and down the course of an old stream as far as Blatchington pond.

46. Seaford station. This picture is hard to date because the actual building has changed very little since the 1860s.

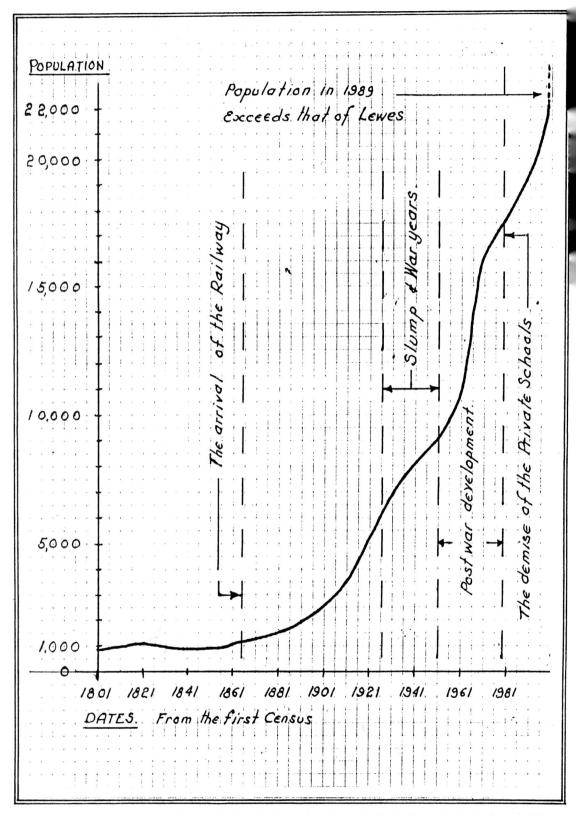

**POPULATION**

22,000
20,000
15,000
10,000
5,000
1,000
0

Population in 1989
exceeds that of Lewes

The arrival of the Railway

Slump & War years.

Post war development.

The demise of the Private Schools.

1801 1821 1841 1861 1881 1901 1921 1941 1961 1981

**DATES.** From the first Census

47. The railway and population. This graph, drawn by the author, shows that Seaford's population in the early 19th century was static and usually under 1,000. The advent of the railway and seaside development increased numbers until the 'slump' and the Second World War. It increased again in post-war years but was slowing down until the availability of the private schools' land for housing gave it further impetus.

# The Old Town

48.   Church Street, *c.*1880. On this drowsy summer lunch time the carter was probably in *The Plough* and the boys were intrigued by the photographer.

49.   Church Street, *c.*1890, this time on a busy afternoon. The tree has now been protected within a pavement.

LYCHGATE AND CHURCH STREET SEAFORD.

50. The lychgate to the church was built in 1896 and the caption to the postcard indicates that it was produced shortly afterwards.

51. A singularly deserted scene photographed from Lower Church Street in a sunny midday with Alma House (Phoenix Corner) on the right, a solitary street lamp and shops now built opposite in South Street.

52. Church Street school, c.1890, from a painting by an unknown artist. This shows the church, the school in its earliest form and a short-lived water tower which dates the picture to between 1889 and 1899.

53.   This card was posted from Seaford in 1938, just a year or two before most of the old buildings on the left were bombed and the character of this narrow little street was destroyed forever.

54. The 'Crypt'. Now only visible as an unsightly lump in the Church Street car park, this is the fine old vaulted undercroft of a 13th-century building, possibly the original town hall. It has two stairs up to ground level and the remains of a further flight to an upper floor. Seldom seen, or even known of by the public, this unique medieval Seaford building is in danger of final dereliction.

55. Church Street around the 1920s. Seen from the lychgate, this shows the narrow entry to West Street on the right and, on the left, Alma House on the corner of South Street. The so-called Crypt was in the gardens behind the buildings by the little motor car. The police station occupies most of this view today.

56.  Church Street in Edwardian times with only pedestrians in sight. The shops with the rather untidy awnings were
J. Martin's tea exchange.

57.  J. Martin advertisement from an Edwardian guide to the town.

GO TO

# J. MARTIN,

## THE SEAFORD

## *TEA EXCHANGE*

AND

### Public Supply Stores,

### 3, ✤ CHURCH ✤ ROAD

*(Near the Railway Station),*

~~❧ S E A F O R D , ❧~~

### for Best Value in

| CHINA, | LAMPS, |
|---|---|
| GLASS, | BRUSHES, |
| EARTHENWARE, | BROOMS, |
| IRONMONGERY, | DOOR MATS, |
| TIN WARE, | BASKETS |

58.  Church Street, *c*.1930. The motor car is now more in evidence but as yet there is no problem parking in mid-afternoon.

59. St Leonard's church. The earliest parts of the church are 11th- and 12th-century, including the Norman columns and carved capitals seen here in the foreground. Alterations were made in the 15th century but the east end and transepts with their brick banding are Victorian. This picture, showing the flat false ceiling to the nave, was probably taken in the very late 19th century.

60. Drawing by M. A. Lower. In 1780 the church had no chancel east of the nave. This picture was evidently drawn about 1850, before the Victorian additions of 1862. The quaint little chancel of no recognisable style must have been quite short lived.

61. Lower High Street, *c*.1880. Seen from the junction with South Street, The Old House, second on the left after Towner Stores, was built in 1650.

62. Laying Seaford's first drains in Lower High Street. This is an almost identical view to the previous sketch. The pedimented door of No.12 (Pelham Bookshop) is just visible on the right where the buildings curve away.

63. Upper High Street, *c*.1900. The *Old Tree Inn*, run by the Swain family in the 18th century, shows little evidence of its 17th-century origin except perhaps for its tiled roof peeping above regimented Victorian facings. The pillory stood outside this building for many years.

64. Upper High Street, *c*.1885. This is a perfect example of the genuine old Seaford and the humble homes of the majority of its inhabitants, little changed from the time when it was the 'pocket borough' of the Duke of Newcastle.

65. Pelham Road, showing very different houses from those seen in Plate 64. The building on the right is West House and the ugly Victorian terraces date from the late 19th century. The shops on the left quickly failed and were converted into private houses soon after they were built.

66. Pelham Place with the station on the left. These dour buildings backed on to the old town and blocked it off from the sea and the view to the south west. The land in front remained vacant until the Ritz cinema was built there in 1936, to be followed by Safeways in the 1980s.

67. Looking up Broad Street from the *Old Tree Inn* (on the right). None of the trees and few of the buildings remain except for the probing spire of the Congregational church, built in 1877. The distance to the spire is about the same as the length of the proposed pier of 1893 (No.9).

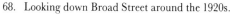

68. Looking down Broad Street around the 1920s.

69. Gable End. This house was built on the south corner of Broad Street and Place Lane in about 1603, contemporary with Sir William Gatwicke's Place House on the north side of the same junction. Place House was demolished in 1936.

70. Gable End in 1950 shortly before it was pulled down. This early 17th-century house had already been despoiled before demolition.

71. Sutton Road, *c*.1920. Until the turn of the century this was the main road out of Seaford to Alfriston and Eastbourne and was still flanked on each side by fields (see Map 5). The Empire cinema was built in 1912 before the great cinema age of Art Deco.

72. Two generations of the Chambers family at the house on Pigeonhouse Farm off Sutton Road. Note the interesting neo-classical window frames in the otherwise rustic timber cladding.

73. Clinton Place: one of the earliest terrace developments in the 19th century and, at least in the engraving, more sympathetic to the old town than Pelham Place. This road stopped at Broad Street at this time. The windmill is Sutton Mill, portrayed with artistic licence concerning its location (see Maps 4 & 5).

74. Clinton Place, 1901. Crowds have gathered to hear the proclamation of the accession of Edward VII read from the balcony of the U.D.C.

75. The proclamation being read.

76. Clinton Place, *c*.1912. Although now developed on both sides (with much less sympathy on the north), the trees stand proudly in the roadway for the convenience of pedestrians, who nevertheless walk in the road because the only traffic is a bicycle, two handcarts and a perambulator! In spite of this, Clinton Place has now supplanted Sutton Road as the main route out to the west.

Terminus Buildings and Clinton Place, Seaford.

77. Clinton Place, *c*.1930. Victorian balconies have now gone, shop signs and fascias project over the pavements and increasing traffic has depleted the number of trees.

78. The old town hall. The steps led up to the court house where the corporation met, the bailiff and jurats dispensed justice and *very* public voting took place at parliamentary elections. Below was the gaol where offenders and even 'pressed' men were confined to await their fate.

79. Coronation Gate. This Tudor arch, now in the wall of Crouch Gardens, was removed from the basement of the old town hall when that historic building was altered beyond recognition. The gate commemorates the coronation of Queen Elizabeth II.

80. The last 'Sergeant of Mace'. William Woolgar, held the office in 1885/6 when the corporation ended. In the 18th century the Sergeant was paid 14s. (70p) each year by the bailiff for 'an hatt'. One of Woolgar's forebears in 1735 built a house on the public highway. He was fined only 5s. and then given a 99-year lease at a peppercorn rent!

81.  Rose Cottage was built in 1650 at much the same time as the 'Old House' in High Street. On the right is the old town hall just before it was damaged by fire in 1989.

82.  Alma House, officially listed as a late 18th-century building. Apart from the shop window, it retains its original fenestration.

83. 'Up the Yard', opposite Alma House. These old stables with accommodation above were built after 1880 and probably about 1890. The picture was taken when the access balconies were still in place.

84. Stone's House, seen next to the modern Seaford House. This house was built in 1767 by Robert Stone (seven times bailiff) in anticipation, it was said, of his marriage to Elizabeth Farncombe, daughter of the man who opposed his election as bailiff in 1762!

85. Old Seaford House, Crouch Lane. There have now been three buildings of the same name on this site. Tennyson is reputed to have written his funeral ode to the Duke of Wellington here.

86. Pear Tree Cottage, Saxon Lane. Listed as an 18th-century building, it was constructed when the road was known as Dark Lane – earlier still it had been Hangman' Lane.

87. Pear Tree Cottage recently photographed to show the surprising height of this charming old house from the garden elevations.

88.  Saxon Lodge, opposite Pear Tree Cottage, was built in 1731. It was once owned by the Beane family who were bailiffs under Charles I and later Charles II, and in the 19th century by the Crook family and briefly by the Chambers family.

89.  A recent picture of Saxon Lodge taken from the garden. Compare with No.129. .

90. Claremont Road in the early days before it was divided by roads leading off to the right.

# The Cuckmere Station

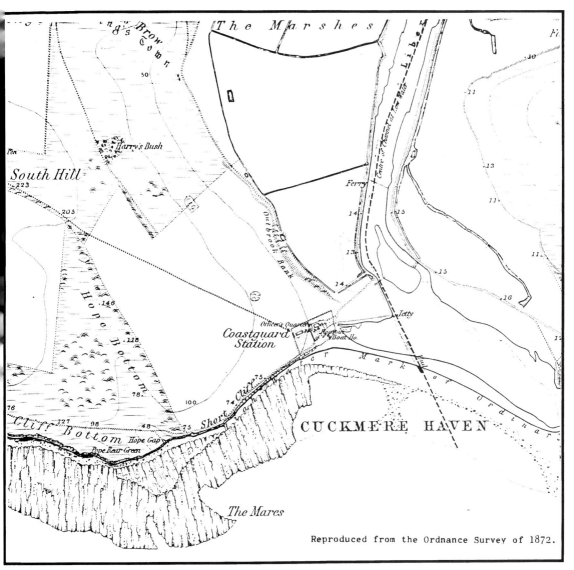

91.  The Cuckmere coastguard station (map of 1872). This station, with officers' quarters, flagstaff and boat house, was built about the same time as the Martello Tower. It would seem to have been a naval concern in the 19th century for a stone in Seaford churchyard records that Lt. Frederick Phillips R.N., buried in 1856, was 'for 23 years in Command of the Cuckmere Station'.

*Cuckmere Haven, near Seaford*

92.   The coastguard station seen from the Cuckmere estuary. This illustrates the enormous cliff erosion that has occurred even since this picture was taken in the early days of this century. The buildings are now perilously close to the cliff edge.

93. Cuckmere coastguard station looking towards the Seven Sisters with two coastguards wearing the rig of a rating and a petty officer.

94. Today, the coastguard (here seen with his telescope) would be dangerously near or even over the cliff!

# Edwardian Advertisements

95-104. The following advertisements all appeared in the same Edwardian guide to the town.

# Blatchington

105.   Blatchington, *c.*1891. On the right is the old *Star Inn* which dates from about 1730, where in the 1747 election the Gages of Firle obtained their drinks to entertain their voters as the Seaford inns were too pro-Pelham to serve them! On the left can be seen the spire of St Peter's church.

106. Blatchington, *c.*1900. The little building on the left is part of the old bakery. Posts have appeared in the road to protect the front of the tall building, the old Rectory, and opposite this is The Gables which on old maps is also designated as 'Rectory'.

107. This view of the village shows, on the right, Rectory Cottage, Glebe Cottage and The Gables. A solitary street lamp has appeared and possibly the beginnings of Homefield Road in the foreground on the right.

108. Blatchington around the 1920s. The *Star Inn* has now been converted into a substantial residence with a new chimney stack added and the windows facing the road filled in. Although the street lamp has now gone there is a pavement on the left and Homefield Road is just visible beyond the *Star*.

109. Blatchington, *c.*1918, looking south with The Gables on the left, the Old Rectory on the right and the old *Star Inn* on the left in the distance.

110. A sketch of the old mill at Blatchington seen on the skyline in the 1785 painting from the sea shore (Plate 14). The mill was in open fields a quarter of a mile north of Blatchington church.

# Storms and Wrecks

111. The storm of 1875, looking across the sea shore from West House to Corsica Hall. The sea has breached the shingle bank, sweeping bathing machines and debris down to the town. The painting hangs in Seaford Museum.

112.   Another painting of the 1875 storm showing boats on the waves in Church Street. Although perhaps more artistic than strictly accurate, the sea did flood almost to the church and behind Seaford Head almost to Chyngton Farm.

113-117. The next five photographs show The Steyne from West House to beyond Saxon Lane in the aftermath of the 1875 floods. Note the debris in the final picture of the sequence which nearly obscures the entry to Saxon Lane by the bow of the boat.

118.  The floods of 1949. Despite a sea wall, this was the temporary state of the Steyne 74 years after the great storm of 1875.

119.  The wreck of the *Gannet* in 1882. Although a steam ship, this vessel was driven ashore near the Martello Tower. Fortunately the crew and cargo were saved.

S.S. GANNET (301, 6)
FROM CALCUTTA TO LONDON. Captain R. WHITE.
RAN ON SHORE 14 FEBRUARY 1882. ONE MAN WAS DROWNED.
PASSENGERS LANDED AT SOUTHAMPTON.
CARGO.
Tea, Coffee, Wheat, Linseed, Cotton, Indigo, Hides and Horns.
SOLD AND BROKENUP.

Propellor Shaft of `S.S. Gannet` Wrecked Feb.14.1882.

Recovered Oct. 1913. By T. Funnell.

120.   The propeller shaft of the *Gannet*, recovered from the sea bed 31 years after the wreck.

121.  The *Peruvian*, wrecked in 1889. This Danish barque was stranded close to the *Esplanade Hotel* and her crew rescued by rocket and breeches buoy. Three days later she was broken up by Atlantic gales. Note the force of the waves breaking over her starboard bow.

122.  The wreck of the *Peruvian* being watched from the promenade. The figurehead (restored in 1989) and some of her cargo of palm nuts are on display in the Seaford Museum.

123.   The *Sagatun* wrecked in 1900. This barque was stranded near the Martello Tower and again the crew and most of the cargo were saved. These were some of the more fortunate of the many ships wrecked in Seaford Bay.

# Telsemaure
# and The Crook Family

124. The Honourable Artillery Company on summer exercises at Seaford in 1858. Amongst them were Thomas Crook and his son Lewis T. Crook who were so impressed with the town that they bought land and in 1860 a large house was built on the sea front for the family. The house was called 'Telsemaure' from the initial letters of family names.

125. Telsemaure, c.1880 (see Map 4). Looking small in isolation, this splendid house had eight bedrooms, four reception rooms, a large playroom, two kitchens and a school room. The gardens, battlemented after the 1875 floods, enclosed lawns, five greenhouses and a museum. There were also roomy stables with accommodation above for staff.

126.  Major Crook on the left with his mother and father and family at Telsemaure. His mother, in the centre, died in 1901 aged 93 and was much mourned in the town.

127. Five generations of the Crook family with Major L. T. Crook on the right. Major Crook was the penultimate bailiff of Seaford in 1884 and his father started the local gas company. His mother (in the picture) was much respected as a generous benefactor, regularly giving food and blankets and other help to the needy in the hard Seaford winters.

128. Major Crook driving his mother and liveried coachman. The coachman and his son, the groom, were members of the Costick family. The Major's mother laid the foundation stone of the Congregational church in 1877 and was affectionately known as 'The Queen of Seaford'.

129.  In 1882 the Major moved into Saxon Lodge where he lived with his own family of nine children. He had a tame raven which perched on his shoulder for regular pre-breakfast walks to see his mother at Telsemaure. When the children married, the Major left Seaford and Saxon Lodge was occupied for a time by the Chambers family.

130.  Major Crook leaving Saxon Lodge with his youngest daughter Gertrude on her wedding day.

131. Sunday School treat. The Major was superintendent of the Congregational Sunday School (as well as president of the local football and cricket teams) and this is a typical picture of many entertainments at Telsemaure.

132. A portrait of Major L. T. Crook wearing full ceremonial uniform of the H.A.C. and the long-service medal bestowed on him by Edward VII at Buckingham Palace.

# Beside the Seaside

133.   The *Esplanade Hotel*, 1905. An interested little crowd gathered outside the hotel when Edward VII paid a visit.

134. Beach entertainers – pierrots can just be seen in the centre of the crowd.

135. Bathing machines. These discreet changing cabins were pulled up and down the beach to allow direct entry into the water whatever the state of the tide.

136.  Bathing and boating. Apart from the bathing machines and local fishing (note the lobster pots and baskets by the sea wall), boats could be hired or trips taken in the bay in small sailing boats.

137.  George and William Templeman, c.1900, two local boatmen and bathing machine operators from an old Seaford family. Back in 1762 another William Templeman was paid 16d. (6½p) by the bailiff 'for beating a drum' to celebrate George III's declaration of war with Spain.

138. Sam Simmons, *c.*1950, from another generation of local boatmen. Sam was then 73 and had worked for 66 years. He said that many years earlier he had taken Winston Churchill out in a boat, possibly when Winston's future wife Clementine was staying in Pelham Place in 1895-99.

139. The Esplanade looking east. In the foreground is the Martello Tower, now tea rooms and roller skating rink. Beyond is the old *Splash Point Hotel*. Note the safe, wide carriageway leading up towards the Head which is now almost totally eroded.

140-144. The next five illustrations are all postcards sent from Seaford between 1914 and 1920.

ROUGH SEA, SPLASH POINT, SEAFORD. 637.

Beach looking Towards Newhaven, Seaford

The Terminus
Emporium.
Seaford.

# The Last Phase

145. Aerial view of Seaford, *c.*1930, showing the sea shore from the Salts to Seaford Head and inland from the railway to Chyngton Farm. Although Telsemaure can still be seen on the outward curve of the Esplanade in the foreground (it was demolished in 1937), there is still little real development west of Pelham Road or to the east of the old town.

146. Sutton Place. Once owned by the Harison family, this house was taken over by the Canadians in World War One and later became Ashampstead School (No.11 on Map 10).

147. Aerial view of King's Mead School and playing fields (No.17 on Map 10). Southdown School is just visible across the Firle Road at the top of the picture.

148. St Peter's School (No.12 on Map 10), seen from the gates in the Alfriston Road. The school closed in 1982, not long before one of its old boys, Col. H. Jones, was awarded a posthumous Victoria Cross in the Falklands War. His name was added to the school's roll of honour which is now in Seaford Museum.

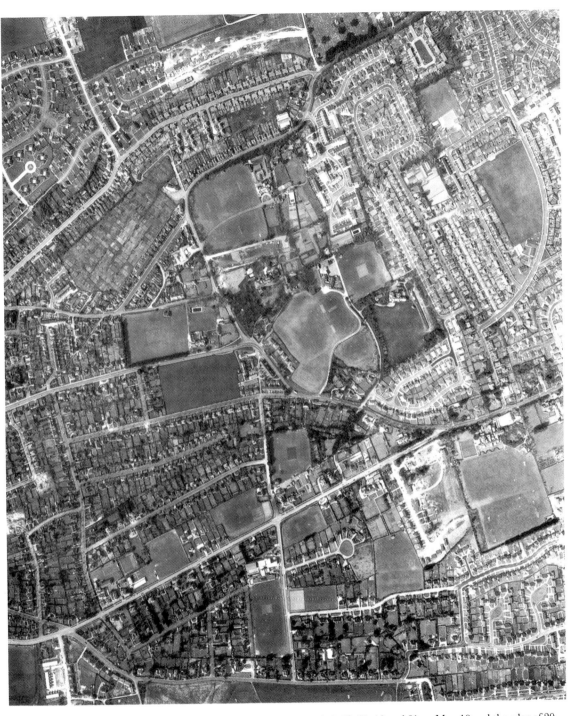

149. Aerial photograph, 1967. The schools numbered 1, 2, 4, 5, 7, 8, 9, 10, 11, 12 and 21 on Map 10 and the edge of 20 can all still be seen as open playing fields in 1967.

# Our Present Link with the Past

Some of these buildings are now 'listed' but none are totally secure from development.

150. The north side of the Steyne in 1989. This townscape is still predominantly made up of buildings of the 19th century or earlier. It defines the southern edge of the old town and is surely worth preserving.

151. The Steyne about 100 years ago.

152. The same scene in 1989. There have been architectural changes, not always for the better but it is still recognisable in form and scale from the early townscape.

153-57. The next five photographs show the individual buildings forming the panorama of No.150.

158.   West House in Pelham Road.

159.   Early 19th-century houses in Lower Church Street.

160.  Albion House, No.2 High Street, built *c*.1714.

161.  Nos.12, 14 and 16 High Street. No.12 is mid-18th-century.

162. The Regency Restaurant, No.20 High Street, was built in the early 19th century, as its name suggests.

163. The Old House, built in 1650.

164. No.45 High Street. Although considered altered, this was built earl

165. Nos.1-3 Crouch Lane, built early in the 19th century or perhaps earlier.

166. A terrace of houses in Church Lane off Church Street ... churchyard. They were built in the mid-19th

167. Behind the *Victoria Sea Hotel*. This jumble of rear extensions to the Victorian seafront terraces is not wonderful architecture, but it is a link with the town's seaside past – a link which could shortly be severed with another drastic degrading of the historic character of the town of Seaford.

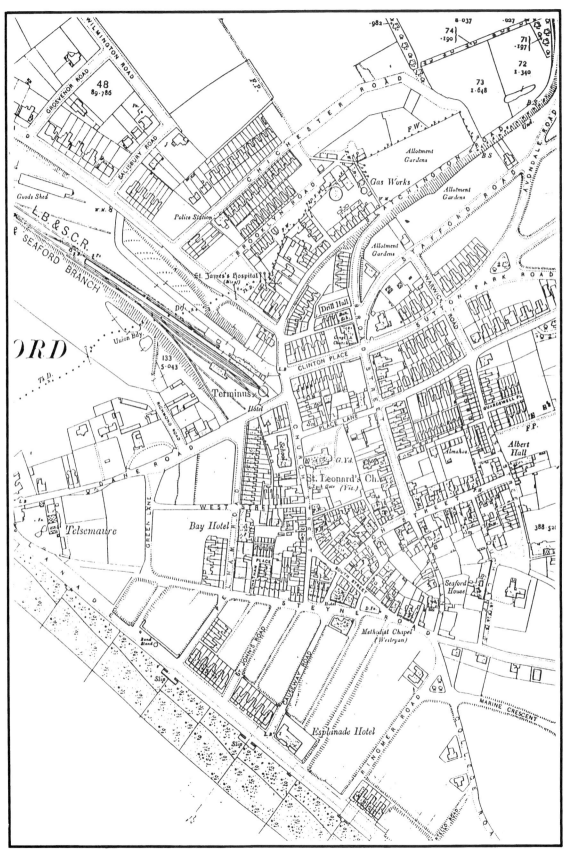

Seaford on the Ordnance Survey map of 1909.